❧ PROFILES OF GREAT ❧
BLACK AMERICANS

Book of Firsts: Leaders of America

❧❧

Edited by Richard Rennert
Introduction by Coretta Scott King

Ⅲ A Chelsea House
Ⅲ Multibiography

Chelsea House Publishers
New York   Philadelphia

Copyright © 1994 by Chelsea House Publishers, a division of
Main Line Book Co. All rights reserved. Printed and bound in the
United States of America.

First Printing

1 3 5 7 9 8 6 4 2

Library of Congress Cataloging-in-Publication Data

   Book of firsts: leaders of America/edited by Richard Rennert;
introduction by Coretta Scott King.
      p. cm.—(Profiles of great black Americans)
Summary: A collection of short biographies of black leaders of
America, including Blanche Bruce, Benjamin Davis, Thurgood
Marshall, and Colin Powell.
   ISBN   0-7910-2065-7
             0-7910-2066-5 (pbk.)
      1. Afro-Americans—Biography—Juvenile literature. 2. Afro-
American leadership—Juvenile literature. [1. Afro-Americans—
Biography. 2. Afro-American—Leadership.] I. Rennert, Richard
Scott, 1956–   . II. Series.
93-25878   E185.96.B62 1993
973'.0496073—dc20   CIP
[B]   AC

❧ CONTENTS ❧

❧ INTRODUCTION ❧
by Coretta Scott King

This book is about black Americans who served society through the excellence of their achievements. It forms a part of the rich history of black men and women in America—a history of stunning accomplishments in every field of human endeavor, from literature and art to science, industry, education, diplomacy, athletics, jurisprudence, even polar exploration.

Not all of the people in this history had the same ideals, but I think you will find something that all of them had in common. Like Martin Luther King, Jr., they all decided to become "drum majors" and serve humanity. In that principle—whether it was expressed in books, inventions, or song—they found something outside themselves to use as a goal and a guide. Something that showed them a way to serve others, instead of only living for themselves.

Reading the stories of these courageous men and women not only helps us discover the principles that we will use to guide our own lives but also teaches us about our black heritage and about America itself. It is crucial for us to know the heroes and heroines of our history and to realize that the price we paid in our struggle for equality in America was dear. But we must also understand that we have gotten as far as we have partly because America's democratic system and ideals made it possible.

We are still struggling with racism and prejudice. But the great men and women in this series are a tribute to the spirit of our democratic ideals and the system in which they have flourished. And that makes their stories special and worth knowing.

BLANCHE K. BRUCE

Political leader Blanche K. Bruce was born Branch Kelso Bruce in Farmville, Virginia, on March 1, 1841. He was one of eleven children of Polly, a slave owned by Lemuel Bruce, a prosperous plantation owner. When Branch was still a baby, one of Lemuel Bruce's heirs took Polly and her children, along with the other slaves, to a farm in Missouri. There the older slaves did farm chores and were hired out to work in brick and tobacco factories. Slaves too young to work, including Branch, played with the children of the master and learned to read and write.

During the years of Branch Bruce's childhood he also lived as a slave on plantations owned by the master's family in both Virginia and Mississippi. By the time he was 15, Branch was once again in Missouri, where he was apprenticed for a while to a printer. Later he was allowed to farm a piece of his own land on the family plantation, and also made rails with other slaves. In 1861, when Kansas was admitted to the Union as a free (nonslave) state, Branch Bruce gained his freedom by moving to Lawrence, Kansas, where he soon changed his first name to Blanche.

For several years Blanche Bruce taught black children at an elementary school he had helped establish in Lawrence. One night in August 1863 a group of proslavery raiders from Missouri descended upon the town, maiming and killing both black and white residents as they looted and burned. Bruce narrowly escaped, and memories of the harrowing event remained with him for the rest of his life. As Bruce saw buildings being burned around him, he made a pledge to himself. He knew that if there were ever to be unity between the races, it had to come about with brains, not torches. Bruce believed that one day there would be a need for black people in positions of leadership, and with the desire to gain more education, he promised himself he would be ready.

He continued to teach at his school for another year, returning to Missouri in early 1865 following that state's passage of an emancipation law. Bruce settled in Hannibal, where he founded the first public school for blacks in the state. As his students increasingly challenged Bruce, he realized that he needed further education. An old friend who was attending Oberlin College, an integrated institution near Cleveland, Ohio, encouraged Bruce to apply. Bruce enrolled at Oberlin, where he became the outstanding student in his class and excelled in mathematics. After a year, however, his money had run out, and his requests to the college for financial aid were turned down. He then moved to St. Louis, where he worked at various trades for a year before traveling farther south into Arkansas and Tennessee.

Increasingly, Bruce heard stories of new opportunities for black Americans in the Deep South, who were now guaranteed the right to vote under the newly passed Reconstruction Acts. In several southern states black Americans made up the majority of the population, and they were slowly beginning to exercise political power. In Mississippi in 1868, 17 freed slaves had joined 49 white men to form a group that wrote a new constitution for the state.

In that same year, Bruce visited Mississippi at the invitation of Samuel Ireland, a prominent black leader whom Bruce had met in St. Louis. Ireland introduced Bruce to James L. Alcorn, a former slave owner who was running for governor. Both Ireland and Alcorn encouraged Bruce to move to Mississippi, and in 1869 he settled on a farm in Floreyville, where he became a successful planter and quickly acquired considerable landholdings. Bruce also became active in Republican party politics, and following the inauguration of James Alcorn as governor in 1870 Bruce was appointed to Alcorn's personal staff. Bruce was especially impressed by Alcorn's promise in his inaugural address to gain full equality for black men in the state.

During the next few years Bruce became prominent in state politics. He held appointed offices of increasing importance, including superintendent of schools for Bolivar County, and then sought elective office. He became county sheriff in 1872 and two years later was elected by the state legislature to serve in the U.S. Senate. Bruce's election as a senator attracted public attention throughout the country, and even the *New York Times* praised Bruce's election in an editorial that lauded his intelligence and "irreproachable private character."

Bruce took his Senate seat in March 1875. With the support of influential Republican members, he was appointed to several important Senate committees, including Education and Labor. During his six years in the Senate, Bruce was a strong supporter of minority rights, including those of the American Indian, and he strongly opposed the exclusion of Chinese workers. He also took a special interest in legislation that strengthened navigation of the Mississippi and worked for the implementation of a flood-control program along the river.

One of Bruce's fellow senators was Lewis V. Bogy, who represented Missouri. Many years earlier, when Bruce was still in his teens and visiting St. Louis, Bogy had asked Bruce to carry his heavy valise down to the docks, then refused to pay him as promised for the service. Now both men were serving together in the Senate, and Bogy needed Bruce's support for a bill. Bruce refused to give him automatic support, reminding him of the incident many years earlier. Bogy quickly apologized and offered payment with interest, but Bruce declined, saying that he would support the bill only if Bogy could convince him of its merits. The two men became close friends and their relationship continued until Bogy's death some years later.

By 1880 the Democratic party controlled the Mississippi state legislature, and Bruce, who was the first black to serve a full term as senator, was not reelected to a second term. Two years earlier he had married Josephine Wilson, a schoolteacher from Cleveland, and the couple had an infant son. They now decided to remain in Washington rather than returning to Bruce's home state. Bruce hoped that the newly elected Republican president, James Garfield, whom he had strongly supported, would name him to an important government post.

Garfield tried to persuade Bruce to accept an appointment as ambassador to Brazil, but Bruce declined on the grounds that slavery was still legal in that country. Bruce also refused an appointment as an assistant to the postmaster general and requested instead that the president name him register of the treasury. His wish was granted and in May 1881 Blanche Bruce was confirmed by the Senate for this position. It was the highest political appointment that a black American had ever received.

At that time the U.S. Treasury Department employed more blacks than all other government departments combined, and Bruce is believed to have chosen this position because of the opportunity it offered to serve other members of his race. The position of register was also prestigious in its own right: Bruce's signature now became one of three that appeared on every piece of paper money printed in the country.

Bruce held the position of register for four years, until the inauguration of a Democrat, Grover Cleveland, in 1885. During the next four years, Bruce became a popular lecturer on a variety of topics, including race relations and education, and toured the country giving speeches that were widely praised. Following the election of the Republican Benjamin Harrison in 1888, Bruce received another political appointment, this time as recorder of deeds for the District of Columbia, which lasted until Cleveland's reelection in 1892. During the early 1890s Bruce also served as a member of the Washington, D.C., school board and in 1894 became a member of the board of trustees of Howard University, which had awarded him an honorary degree a year earlier.

In March 1897, following the inauguration of Republican president William McKinley, Bruce asked the president for his old job as register of the treasury.

However, it took months for McKinley to respond, and Bruce was not sworn in until December 1897. He died three months later, on March 17, 1898, as a result of chronic diabetes and kidney disease.

The black race and all of Washington mourned the passing of Blanche Bruce with his family and friends. The *Boston Herald* reported: "The death of Blanche K. Bruce, Register of the Treasury, removes one of the strong men of the colored race in this country. He was not so popular among his own people as he deserved to be, but he enjoyed the confidence of those who knew him without regard to color." Bruce once said, "I have diligently sought to be advised of the will and wants of the people of my state, that I might faithfully represent one and effectually meet the others. . . . Appreciating my obligation to my race, I have sought impartially and justly to ascertain and subserve the interests of all classes of the citizens of Mississippi."

RALPH BUNCHE

Diplomat and Nobel Peace Prize winner Ralph Bunche was born in Detroit, Michigan, on August 7, 1904. He was the descendant of slaves and also had several Native American ancestors. Bunche's father was a barber and his mother a musician. When Ralph was 10 years old, the family moved to Albuquerque, New Mexico, because Mrs. Bunche, who was ill, needed to live in a dry climate.

However, in 1916 both of Ralph's parents died, and he was sent to Los Angeles to be raised by his maternal grandmother.

When Ralph Bunche was attending school, his grandmother received a note on his report card that he was unruly in class. She went to see the principal and asked if her grandson was being given courses that would prepare him for college. The principal said no; like all black children, Ralph was enrolled in practical commercial courses which would prepare him for a job after finishing school. Bunche's grandmother insisted that he was going to college no matter what the cost and the school should prepare him for it. Although the principal argued that few white children, let alone blacks, attended college, he changed Bunche's curriculum to academic courses and he graduated in 1922 with highest honors from Jefferson High School, where he was class valedictorian.

The school principal congratulated Bunche's grandmother on his achievements. He commented that he did very well in academics and athletics and that the school had never thought of him as a Negro. To this, his grandmother said, "Why not? He *is* a Negro and proud of it. So am I. What you have just said is an insult to Ralph, to me, to his parents, and the whole race. . . ." Ralph later said, "success, I must confess, had a sweeter taste because of color."

Bunche received several scholarships to the University of California at Los Angeles (UCLA), where he majored in international relations. He supported himself by working as a janitor and doing other odd jobs.

At UCLA Bunche distinguished himself as both a student and an athlete. He was the star guard on three championship basketball teams and also played baseball and football. In addition, he became a skilled debater and orator. During his undergraduate years, Bunche developed an interest in race relations, a field in which he would later become an expert.

Bunche graduated with highest honors from UCLA in 1927 and was elected to Phi Beta Kappa, the national honor society. Delivering the valedictory address, Bunche spoke of respecting each person's rights. He said our basic dilemma is that "Man *learns* and *knows* but he does not *do* as well as he knows." He told the audience to "Look up, not down, look out, not in, and lend a hand. . . vision is the quality which all men may have in common. It is that 'bigness' of soul and heart which enables man to understand—to understand and love his fellows."

Residents of his neighborhood raised $1,000 so that Bunche could continue his education, and that fall he enrolled at Harvard University. In 1928, after receiving a master of arts degree in government from Harvard, Bunche began teaching political science at Howard University in Washington, D.C. While there he married Ruth Harris, one of his students, and they eventually had three children. Bunche became a full professor at Howard and chairman of the political science department.

After four years at Howard, Bunche returned to Harvard in 1932 to earn his Ph.D. in government. A fellowship from the university allowed him to do research in Africa for his dissertation, a comparative study of the governments of French Togoland (now the Republic of Togo) and Dahomey (now Benin). Instead of using official government reports for his research, Bunche traveled with natives into the interiors of both countries and personally observed conditions there. Bunche's dissertation received a prize from the Harvard faculty and earned him the Ph.D. in 1934.

Bunche returned to Howard to teach for several years. Then, in 1936–37, on a fellowship from the Social Science Research Council, he did further study at the London School of Economics and at the University of Capetown in South Africa. He also traveled extensively in East Africa and lived for three months with the Kikuyu tribe in Kenya as an honorary tribal citizen. Returning to the United States, Bunche traveled around the world via Malaya, the Philippines, China, Japan, and Hawaii.

Bunche's first long publication on race relations, a booklet entitled *A World View of Race*, was issued in 1937 by the Progressive Education Association. He also published a number of articles on the subject in several periodicals. From 1938 to 1940 Bunche was on leave from Howard University to serve on the staff of the Carnegie Corporation in New York City. During these years, he worked as chief assistant to Gunnar Myrdal, a prominent Swedish sociologist who was studying the conditions of black Americans. The two often traveled together, and several times they were driven out of towns in the South by angry residents who accused them of "stirring up trouble." Myrdal later published the results of his research in a book called *An American Dilemma* (1944), long considered a classic study of race relations in the United States.

In 1941, as World War II raged in Europe and Asia, Bunche again obtained a leave from Howard University so that he could work as a policy analyst for the U.S. government. He served in the Office of Strategic Services (OSS) as an expert on Africa and the Far East and advised the Joint Chiefs of Staff on colonial areas around the world. After several years with the OSS, Bunche joined the U.S. Department of State as a specialist on colonial affairs. He received several promotions and for a time served as acting chief of the Division of Dependent Area Affairs—the first African American to hold the post of acting chief in any State Department office.

In 1945 Bunche was an adviser to the U.S. delegation attending the Conference on International Organization in San Francisco. This was the meeting that led to the formation of the United Nations. Earlier, Bunche had written sections for the organization's charter on the governing of former colonies. After the war he served as a U.S. representative to the UN General Assembly, which met in London, and also represented his country at major conferences in Europe and America.

Bunche joined the Secretariat of the United Nations in 1946 as director of the Trusteeship Division, which he had helped to organize. A year later he was sent to the Middle East as a representative of the United Nations Special Committee on Palestine. In December 1947 he became principal secretary of the UN Palestine Commission. Bunche would have preferred to continue in the Trusteeship Division, which oversaw lands that had been colonies prior to World War II. However, he realized that the resolution of conflict in Palestine was an important issue that he could not ignore.

At the heart of the Palestine conflict was warfare between Jews and Arabs, both of whom lived in the region. For many years the region of Palestine had been ruled by Great Britain. After World War II Britain agreed to let the United Nations decide Palestine's future. In 1947 the UN voted to divide the region into separate Arab and Jewish states. Civil war broke out as Jews and Arabs fought over territory.

In his role with the UN Palestine Commission, Bunche became a major figure in resolving the Arab-Jewish dispute. When the UN–appointed mediator, Count Folke Bernadotte, was assassinated in September 1948, Bunche became acting mediator in the conflict. He eventually brought about an armistice between the new Jewish state of Israel and the surrounding Arab states. In recognition of his efforts, Bunche was awarded the 1950 Nobel Peace Prize— the first African American to receive a Nobel Prize.

Bunche continued as an official of the UN Secretariat following his resolution of the Palestine conflict. In 1955 he was named an under secretary of the UN and two years later became under secretary for special political affairs, a post he held until 1967. In that year Bunche was named under secretary general of the United Nations and continued in that position until his retirement four years later. During this time Bunche directed successful peacekeeping efforts in the Suez Canal Zone (1956), the Congo (1964), and Cyprus (1964). He died in New York City on December 9, 1971, leaving behind an unparalleled legacy of dedication to the cause of world peace.

SHIRLEY CHISHOLM

Shirley Chisholm, America's first black congresswoman, was born Shirley Anita St. Hill on November 20, 1924, in the Bedford-Stuyvesant section of Brooklyn, New York. She was the oldest of Ruby and Charles St. Hill's four daughters. Hoping to save money for the girls' education, their parents sent them to live with their grandmother in Barbados in 1927. Seven years later, Shirley and her sisters returned to the United States, which was by then in the grip of the Great Depression.

Like millions of other Americans of the 1930s, the St. Hills had very little money, but they never considered letting a school-age child work. To Charles St. Hill, a fifth-grade dropout himself, education came first. His girls rewarded his faith by doing well at school; Shirley led the pack by graduating at the top of her high school class and receiving scholarship offers from Vassar and Oberlin. Unable to afford a distant school even on a scholarship, Shirley St. Hill enrolled in Brooklyn College, from which she graduated cum laude in 1946.

Urged by her college professors to consider politics as a career, star pupil St. Hill had demurred: "You forget two things," she said. "I'm black—and I'm a woman." After college, she took a job at a Harlem child-care center, where she worked for seven years while studying for a master's degree in early childhood education at Columbia University night school. She received the degree in 1952. During this period, she met and married a recent immigrant from Jamaica, graduate student Conrad Chisholm.

From 1953 to 1964, Shirley Chisholm served as an educational consultant for the New York City Bureau of Child Welfare. Meanwhile, she had finally entered politics. In 1960, the 36-year-old educator, along with a group of reform-minded neighbors, decided to oust the local Democratic political machine and replace it with a new, liberal party organization. Their group, the Unity Democratic Club, failed in its first bid to take over the district, but their second try, in 1962, fared differently.

That year, the Unity Club managed to place two of its candidates on the slate. Both won election to the New York State Assembly, thereby giving control of the 17th Assembly District to the reformers. Two years later, one of these assemblymen became a judge, leaving a vacant slot. Chisholm decided to fill it herself.

After what she later called "a long, hard summer and fall," Shirley Chisholm swept to a win in a three-way contest, racking up 18,151 votes to her nearest opponent's 1,893. She went to Albany, New York's capital, and from 1964 until 1968 served as assemblywoman for the 17th District. During those four years, the Brooklyn woman proved herself a tough, independent politician. Among her accomplishments was the enactment into law of two of her pet projects: SEEK, a program providing college funds for poor youngsters, and an unemployment insurance fund for domestic employees.

After two terms in Albany, Assemblywoman Chisholm turned her eyes toward the nation's capital. A redistricting of her residential area created the new, predominantly black 12th Congressional District. Nominated by an independent citizens' committee, she defeated the party regular for the nomination, then went on to defeat the Republican candidate, Congress of Racial Equality founder James Farmer.

In early 1969, Congresswoman Shirley Chisholm took her seat in the House of Representatives—the first black woman ever to do so.

As a member of the 91st Congress, Chisholm showed herself as independent minded as she had been in the state legislature. When House leaders assigned her to the Agricultural Committee—a post they had assumed she would appreciate because of the committee's jurisdiction over food stamps—Chisholm astonished her colleagues by protesting vehemently. Showing unusual political skill for a congressional freshman, she managed to get herself reassigned, first to the Veterans Affairs Committee, where she served two years, then to her first choice: the powerful Education and Labor Committee. Demonstrating her sentiments—and her strengths—Chisholm helped engineer passage of a number of major bills. Included were laws that aided the poor, increased minimum wages, and created federal subsidies to support daycare centers for working mothers.

In 1970, voters of the 12th Congressional District enthusiastically returned Chisholm to Washington. But as a congresswoman, she soon felt she had pushed her agenda as far as possible. To accomplish what she believed America needed—among other things, a more equitable share of work and power for minorities and women—she decided to aim for the top. In 1972, she announced her candidacy for the Democratic nomination for president of the United States. Never before in the nation's history had a black or a woman—to say nothing of a *black woman*—sought the presidential nomination of a major party.

Chisholm had acquired a core of dedicated campaign workers and supporters, but with limited funds at their disposal, these loyalists made scant headway against the well-financed, well-organized opposition. When Chisholm went to the Democratic National Convention in 1972, she went with only 24 committed delegates. Candidate Hubert Humphrey, aware that he could not block the candidacy of South Dakota's senator George McGovern, released his delegates to Chisholm, but the battle was not even close. McGovern took the nomination, going on to lose the election (by a landslide) to incumbent Richard Nixon.

Despite her failure to capture the presidential nomination, Chisholm looked on the effort as its own kind of triumph. She spoke to reporters after the election:

> In terms of black politics, I think an effect of my campaign has been to increase the independence and self-reliance of many local elected black officials and black political activists from the domination of the political "superstars." The United States was said not to be ready to elect a Catholic to the presidency when Al Smith [Governor Alfred E. Smith of New York, a Democrat and a Roman Catholic, who lost to Republican Herbert Hoover in 1928] ran in the 1920s. But Smith's nomination may have helped pave the way for the successful campaign John F. Kennedy [a Roman Catholic Massachusetts senator] waged in 1960. Who can tell? What I hope most is that now there will be others who will feel

themselves as capable of running for high political office as any wealthy, good-looking white male.

Undiscouraged by her unsuccessful tilt at the presidency, Chisholm sought and easily won reelection to Congress in 1972. By this time, she had gained a secure national reputation for her undeviating advocacy of minority and women's rights. She once said that although she had been the first black woman elected to the U.S. Congress, she wanted to be remembered instead "as a catalyst for change, a woman who had the determination and a woman who had the perseverance to fight on behalf of the female population and the black population, because I'm a product of both."

As the years passed—Chisholm would eventually win and serve a total of seven terms in Congress—the Brooklyn maverick came somewhat closer to joining ranks with the party she represented. But she still resisted party discipline, sticking to her own route when she saw it as best for her constituents. She voted, for example, against several Democratic-backed bills that aimed at protecting the environment, asserting that their immediate result would be job losses among the poor.

In February 1982, Chisholm announced her retirement; she would finish out her term, but she would not be a candidate in November 1982. Supporters reacted with dismay, but many understood that personal reasons played a large role in the congresswoman's decision. In 1977, soon after a quiet divorce from Conrad Chisholm, 52-year-old Shirley Chisholm married Arthur Hardwick, Jr., a black businessman and former New York State assemblyman. Two years after the wedding, Hardwick had almost died in an automobile accident; Chisholm found the conflict between caring for her recovering husband and serving in Congress more than she wished to face. As one observer put it, "Her husband's accident and the new conservative climate in Washington [rightwing Republican Ronald Reagan had been elected in 1980] prompted Shirley to think about her own goals."

After retiring from politics, Chisholm taught political science and women's studies at Mount Holyoke College; she also gave frequent lectures and, in 1985, accepted the post of honorary scholar at Spelman College. Her husband died in 1986, and she gave up her teaching positions shortly afterward. In 1988, she joined Jesse Jackson's campaign for the presidency, just as she had four years earlier.

In the mid-1980s, Chisholm created a new organization, the National Political Caucus of Black Women, which soon counted thousands of members across the United States. An active member of the League of Women Voters, the National Association for the Advancement of Colored People, and the National Board of Americans for Democratic Action, she has also written two autobiographies: *Unbought and Unbossed* and *The Good Fight*.

BENJAMIN O. DAVIS, SR., and
BENJAMIN O. DAVIS, JR.

Military leader Benjamin O.
Davis, Sr., was born on June 1, 1877, in Washington,
D.C. One of his grandfathers was a slave who bought
his freedom in 1800. Davis's father worked as a mes-
senger for the Department of the Interior. Benjamin
Davis attended public schools in Washington, and

as a teenager he often visited Fort Myer, the U.S. Army post across the Potomac River near Arlington, Virginia.

After attending Howard University in Washington, D.C., Davis joined the 8th U.S. Infantry as a first lieutenant in July 1898, during the Spanish-American War. He was mustered out of the infantry the following March, and three months later enlisted in the cavalry of the regular army as a private. Davis was sent to the Philippine Islands, where he served for two years. He was promoted to corporal and then to squadron sergeant major. In February 1901 Davis was commissioned a second lieutenant of cavalry and later that year became adjutant at Fort Washakie, Wyoming.

Following his promotion to first lieutenant in March 1905, Davis became a professor of military science and tactics at Wilberforce University, a black institution in Wilberforce, Ohio. He remained there for four years. In 1909 Davis was sent by the army to Monrovia, Liberia, where he served as military attaché until 1912. He was then assigned to the 9th Cavalry at Fort Russell, Wyoming. The 9th Cavalry later moved to Douglas, Arizona, where it patrolled the U.S.–Mexico border.

In 1915 Davis returned to Wilberforce to teach military science. That same year he was promoted to captain and two years later became an acting major. In the summer of 1917 Davis was again sent to the Philippines, where he served as supply officer of the 9th Cavalry at Camp Stotsenburg. In 1918 Davis was named a temporary lieutenant colonel; two years later the rank became permanent.

From 1920 to 1924 Davis served as a professor of military science and tactics at the Tuskegee Institute, the world-famous educational institution for blacks founded in the late 19th century by Booker T. Washington. In 1924 Davis was sent to Cleveland, Ohio, where he became an instructor in the Ohio National Guard for five years.

In 1929 Davis was ordered to accompany a delegation of mothers and widows of U.S. soldiers to Europe. The soldiers had been killed during World War I, and the women were making a pilgrimage to the cemeteries where they were buried. Upon his return to the United States, Davis was highly commended for his role in this assignment by both the secretary of war and the army's quartermaster general. In 1930 Davis was promoted to colonel.

During the next eight years, Davis taught alternately at Wilberforce and Tuskegee. In 1938 he became commanding officer of the 369th Infantry of the New York National Guard. Two years later, in October 1940, Davis was promoted to brigadier general—the first black American general in the U.S. Army. Davis served as brigade commander with the Second Cavalry Division in Fort Riley, Kansas, for six months before his retirement in June 1941.

Davis was recalled to active duty later that month as assistant to the inspector general in Washington, D.C. In October 1942, 10 months after the United States entered World War II, Davis was sent to

England as an adviser to General Dwight D. Eisenhower, then commanding general of the European Front. Throughout the war Davis advised the general on the use of black soldiers. He worked to ease racial tensions and to end discrimination in all of the armed services.

Davis's years of service between 1941 and 1945 seem to be the most important. With his rank of brigadier general, he showed that blacks can attain positions of authority and leadership. During the time that he worked in the inspector general's office, black soldiers and officers felt that they could speak freely to Davis, and he worked privately with other high ranking blacks in trying to end discrimination in the military. It has been said that the eventual change in the military's policy of segregation came about partly due to Davis's contributions.

As Davis approached his 64th birthday, he was often questioned about retirement, to which he replied: "I think I have done my share but if the War Department desires me to continue to serve in the national emergency, I will have an open mind." Davis retired permanently from the army in 1948 after 50 years of service. He died on November 26, 1970. Davis was married for many years and had three children: two daughters and a son, Benjamin O. Davis, Jr., who was born on December 18, 1912, in Washington, D.C.

Like his father, Benjamin O. Davis, Jr., attended public schools in Washington, D.C. In 1929 he graduated from Central High School in Cleveland, Ohio, where he was president of his class and an outstanding student. Davis junior attended Western Reserve University in Cleveland for one year, then studied mathematics for two years at the University of Chicago. He hoped to become a mathematics teacher, but in 1932 his plans changed when he was offered an appointment to the U.S. Military Academy at West Point, New York.

Although he failed the entrance examinations the first time he took them, Davis junior studied hard and succeeded in his second attempt. During his first year at West Point, he was subjected to a rigorous form of hazing known as the silent treatment. No other cadet spoke to him for an entire year, but Davis junior endured this treatment without complaint and was cheered by his classmates when the year had ended.

Davis graduated in 1936, the first black to do so since 1889. Davis junior then attended Infantry School at Fort Benning, Georgia, and then served for several years as an instructor in military science and tactics at Tuskegee Institute—again following in his father's footsteps. During World War II Davis junior trained as a pilot at the Advanced Army Flying School and served with the Army Air Corps in Italy and North Africa. He received regular promotions and in May 1944 became a full colonel. In September of that year he received the Distinguished Flying Cross—which was pinned on his chest by his father, Brigadier General Benjamin O. Davis, Sr.

In April 1945 Davis junior led an air corps bombing attack on railway targets in Austria. For his bravery he won the army's Silver Star—the first time that a black American fighter pilot had been given that award. After the war Davis became field commander of the 477th Composite Group at Godman Field, Kentucky, the first black American to hold such an important position in the Army Air Corps. From 1946 to 1949 Davis was commander of the Lockbourne Army Air Base.

From 1941 to 1949, Davis experienced eight years of a segregated Army Air Force. In June 1949, Secretary Symington and chief of staff Vandenberg imposed integration on the air force, which surprisingly was an immediate success. According to Davis, "These men had correctly determined that the Air Force would be a better military service in a better nation by the elimination of segregation. The courageous performance of black airmen in World War II helped Symington and Vandenberg immeasurably in making their decision."

In the 1940s, the army reported having one general and 10 colonels as top black officers. While the number of blacks enlisting in the military increased over the years, in 1965 blacks made up less than four percent of officers in the army and two percent in the air force.

In 1949 Davis enrolled at the Air War College in Alabama and graduated a year later. He then joined the staff at the headquarters of the U.S. Air Force in Washington, D.C., where he was named chief of the fighter branch in 1951. In early 1954 he became director of operations and training of the Far East Air Forces.

In October 1954 Davis was promoted to the rank of brigadier general in the air force by President Dwight D. Eisenhower—whom his father had advised when Eisenhower commanded American troops in Europe during World War II. Benjamin O. Davis, Jr., thus became the first black American air force general.

In addition to the Distinguished Flying Cross and the Silver Star, Davis was awarded the Air Medal, with four oak-leaf clusters; the Legion of Merit; and the French Croix de Guerre, with palm. He was elevated to the rank of lieutenant general before retiring from the air force.

WILLIAM H. HASTIE

Judge and educator William H. Hastie was born on November 17, 1904, in Knoxville, Tennessee. He was the only child of William and Roberta Childs Hastie. Young Hastie's father had attended Ohio Wesleyan and Howard universities, where he studied mathematics and pharmacy, but as a black man he was unable to find employment as an actuary or a pharmacist. He eventually found a job with the U.S. government, becoming the first African American to be appointed a clerk in the Pension Office. Roberta Childs Hastie was a schoolteacher who had been educated at Fisk University.

Young William Hastie attended public schools in Knoxville and, after the age of 12, in Washington, D.C., where his father had been transferred. He went on to attend Washington's Dunbar High School, one of the country's leading secondary schools for black students. One of his classmates was Charles Drew, who later became a world-renowned doctor who pioneered the preservation of blood plasma. At Dunbar, students were taught that there was nothing they could not do. They would do well in school, go to college, and enter a profession. Parents of many students pushed them to be academically outstanding.

Hastie graduated from Dunbar at the top of his class in 1921, although the occasion was bittersweet; his father had died suddenly a few months earlier. Fortunately, William and Roberta Hastie had carefully saved money for many years so that their talented son could attend a leading college, and that fall he was able to enroll at Amherst College in Massachusetts.

Blacks at Amherst were not treated with the same respect as white students. They were not allowed opportunities such as joining fraternities or the glee club. Hastie, along with fellow blacks, simply wanted to be given the chance to compete equally with other students. Willing to fight for this, he said, "You with brown skins will not make Chi Phi nor even get bids to fraternity dances, not now. But continue sending more and more representatives of your race against whom no negligibility can be found except the color of their skins, and unless human nature is basically rotten, recognition will come in time."

Hastie majored in mathematics at Amherst, but he took a variety of courses in other fields, including German, Greek, and physics, as well as a class in creative writing with the poet Robert Frost. Hastie also found time for athletics at Amherst and starred as a member of the varsity track team. In 1925 he graduated as the top student in his class. He was elected to Phi Beta Kappa, the national honor society, and later served as president of the Amherst chapter of that organization.

Hastie's high academic standing earned him a fellowship for further study at either the University of Paris or Oxford University in England, but he decided to remain in the United States and earn money so that he could eventually attend law school. For two years Hastie taught mathematics and science at the Bordentown Manual Training School, an institution for black youth in New Jersey. Then, in 1927, he entered Harvard Law School where he excelled in his studies and served as an editor of the *Law Review*.

After graduating near the top of his class in 1930, Hastie joined the faculty of the Howard University Law School in Washington, D.C., which he said was "the one institution to which a colored man at present can look for an opportunity to teach law." In 1931 he began practicing law in Washington and a year later earned a doctorate in law from Harvard University.

In 1933 Hastie began his long career of service with the U.S. government when he became assistant solicitor of the Department of the Interior. Four years later he was appointed judge of the U.S. District Court for the Virgin Islands and thus became the first black person ever appointed to a federal judgeship. This position was especially appropriate for a black appointee because the Virgin Islands then had a population that was 90 percent black.

After his two-year term expired, Hastie returned to Howard University as dean and professor of law. In November 1940 he took a leave of absence from Howard to become an aide to Secretary of War Henry L. Stimson. Hastie's job was to advise Stimson on the role of African Americans in the armed forces. Hastie was successful in his efforts to increase the number of blacks in the army and air force. However, he was dismayed to find that there were few black officers, and that the armed services seemed unwilling to train soldiers for these positions.

At that time, the armed forces were segregated, and whites and blacks did not serve in the same unit. Moreover, white troops were given the more prestigious, skilled jobs, while blacks were assigned to menial labor. Hastie protested the continuation of these policies but he was ignored. Finally, in January 1943 Hastie resigned from the War Department in protest.

Hastie returned to Howard University as a professor and dean of the law school. However, he continued to protest the unfair treatment of blacks in the armed forces, including reports of assaults on black soldiers by white civilians and policemen near bases where they were stationed. Hastie's protests had some positive consequences: in March 1944 army officials ordered that black and white soldiers be trained together at officer candidate schools. Four years later President Harry S Truman issued an executive order ending all forms of segregation in the U.S. armed forces.

Hastie battled segregation in other areas besides the military. He was a leading opponent of the poll tax, a fee that was used to keep poor blacks from voting in the South. The poll tax was finally banned in national elections by the Twenty-fourth Amendment to the U.S. Constitution, which was ratified in 1964. Two years later the U.S. Supreme Court also banned the poll tax in state and local elections. Hastie's vigorous opposition to segregation earned him recognition from several organizations, including the National Association for the Advancement of Colored People (NAACP), which awarded him its prestigious Spingarn Medal in 1943.

In 1946 Hastie was appointed governor of the Virgin Islands by President Truman. He accepted the position of governor because he thought of it as an honor to his race. Hastie had been content with his work at Howard University, and the move to the Virgin Islands transferred him out of the middle of the civil rights battle. Hastie did, however, return to the mainland often in order to remain involved with the civil rights movement.

Although Hastie worked hard to improve conditions in the Virgin Islands and encouraged tourism to bolster the country's faltering economy, he was often frustrated in his role as governor. Hastie was hailed by the people at first—Isdor Paiewonsky, a Virgin Island buisinessman said, "Hastie was such an example of the proper use of political power"—but later was condemned by legislators who believed the governor was not spending his time wisely. The editor of the St. Thomas *Daily News* wrote that although Hastie's first obligation was clearly to the Virgin Islands, "However, there is evidence that he devotes too much of his attention and energy to dealing with racial, educational and political matters on a national scale while his government continues to disintegrate under him."

During the 1948 presidential election, Hastie took a leave of absence to campaign widely for Truman. Following the president's reelection, Hastie was rewarded for his support when Truman named him to a seat on the U.S. Court of Appeals for the Third Circuit. While waiting to be confirmed [by the U.S. Senate] it was said that failure of all members to provide "a prompt, favorable report can only be attributed to the fact that [Hastie] is a Negro." Following his confirmation in July 1950, Hastie became the first black federal judge.

For the rest of his life, Hastie and his family—he had married in 1943 and had a daughter—made their home in Philadelphia, the site of the Third Circuit Court of Appeals. In 1968 Hastie became chief judge of the court and served in that capacity until 1971, when he retired with the title of senior judge. In 1975 he was named that year's recipient of the Philadelphia Award, presented annually to an individual for advancing the "best and largest interest of the community." This unsung pioneer of the civil rights movement died in East Norriton, Pennsylvania, on April 14, 1976.

THURGOOD MARSHALL

The United States Supreme Court justice Thurgood Marshall was born on July 2, 1908, in West Baltimore, Maryland. He was the second son of William, a waiter, and Norma Marshall, a schoolteacher. William Marshall, who had little education but a keen mind, taught young Thurgood how to debate and encouraged him to pursue a legal career. From his mother, Thurgood learned tact and diplomacy. The Marshalls stressed the value of personal dignity and modesty, but they never recommended meekness. "Anyone calls you nigger," said William to Thurgood, "you not only got my permission to fight him—you got my orders to fight him."

Graduating from high school in 1925, Marshall enrolled in Lincoln University, an all-black Philadelphia institution where he became a star debater. In the fall of his senior year, Marshall married University of Pennsylvania student Vivian Burey; the following June, he graduated from Lincoln with honors in the humanities. He entered the law school of Howard University, a black institution in Washington, D.C., in 1930.

At the end of his first year, Howard's professors named Marshall top student in his class. Among the distinguished professors who helped him polish his skills was Charles Hamilton Houston, a brilliant attorney and pioneering civil rights activist. Houston provided legal assistance to the National Association for the Advancement of Colored People (NAACP), an organization founded in 1909 to combat racial discrimination. Marshall often helped him plan strategy for his NAACP cases.

In 1933, Marshall graduated first in his class from Howard Law School. Although Harvard University immediately offered him a postgraduate scholarship, he was eager to begin practicing law and turned it down. After passing the Maryland State law examination, he opened a law office in east Baltimore.

In the grip of the Great Depression (1929–40), few Americans of any race could afford legal representation, and black lawyers had a particularly hard time. In his first year of practice, Marshall had no paying clients, and he often took on the cases of poor people, thereby earning him a reputation as "the little man's lawyer." Preparing for each trial with painstaking care, he won many of his early cases.

Marshall's public service work gained him not only experience but a steadily growing reputation. In 1934, the local chapter of the NAACP named him as its lawyer, an unpaid but exhilarating job. He kicked off his NAACP career by organizing a boycott of white-owned Baltimore stores that sold to blacks in a black neighborhood yet employed only whites. When the shopkeepers responded by suing the NAACP, Marshall teamed up with Charles Houston and successfully defended the organization in federal court.

In 1935, the NAACP began to concentrate on integrating graduate and professional schools. With Houston, Marshall scored his first major court victory when he won a suit against the University of Maryland for refusing to admit blacks to its law school. In 1936, Marshall accepted a job as assistant to Houston, who had become first special counsel at NAACP headquarters in New York City. Defending the rights of black students and teachers in the South, the two men spent the next two years traveling from one southern courthouse to another. Between trips, Marshall continued to help poor clients at his small Baltimore office.

Marshall's first case as assistant special counsel involved the University of Missouri Law School, which had refused to admit a qualified black student. Working with Houston, Marshall used the "separate-but-equal" doctrine in arguing the Missouri case, asserting that the law school had to admit the student unless it could offer "equal" education at an all-black institution. (U.S. courts had been using this doctrine, established by a Supreme Court case known as *Plessy v. Ferguson*, to decide segregation cases since 1896. Basically, *Plessy* allowed racial segregation as long as blacks had access to "equal" or equivalent facilities.)

The Missouri Law School case went all the way to the U.S. Supreme Court, which found in the NAACP's favor by a vote of six to two. The decision meant that Missouri—and other states—now had only two choices: to admit blacks to their all-white, publicly funded schools, or to build and staff brand-new, equal facilities for blacks—an almost impossibly expensive proposition. Elated NAACP officials realized that one day the Supreme Court might extend the doctrine to the nation's public schools at all levels.

In 1939, Marshall, now black America's most prominent attorney, became director-counsel of a new organization: the NAACP Legal Defense and Educational Fund, Inc., a body created to provide free legal aid to blacks who suffered racial injustice. As fund chief, Marshall prepared his first solo Supreme Court brief in 1940. In this case, *Chambers v. Florida*, the NAACP sought to overturn the convictions of a white man. Marshall argued that police officials had wrung confessions from the men after five days of nonstop grilling, and that such "sunrise confessions" violated the U.S. Constitution's guarantee of "due process of law."

Marshall next focused his sights on a notorious device employed to keep southern blacks from voting. In the South, primary winners always won the election. Only party members could vote in the primary, and only whites could belong to the party. Marshall based his 1944 challenge to the "white primary" on the Fifteenth Amendment, which forbids states to deprive citizens of their vote "on account of race, color, or previous condition of servitude." The U.S. Supreme Court upheld Marshall's argument, a decision that sounded the death knell for the South's white primary.

In 1946, the NAACP awarded Marshall its highest award, the Spingarn Medal. By 1948, the 40-year-old lawyer had earned the nickname "Mr. Civil Rights." That same year, he went after unfair housing practices. Arguing before the Supreme Court, Marshall maintained that restrictive covenants—agreements between whites that effectively kept blacks out of white neighborhoods—restricted blacks' rights as Americans. Agreeing, the court struck down the covenants. Two years later Marshall argued and won two major segregation-in-education cases before the Supreme Court. His twin victories led to the admission of black students to the Universities of Oklahoma and Texas, and in 1950 he succeeded in getting a black law student enrolled at Louisiana State University.

In 1952, Marshall and his NAACP team scored one of the organization's most resounding triumphs. After extensive preparation, the lawyers brought *Brown v. Board of Education of Topeka* to the Supreme Court. A combination of five cases from around the country, *Brown* was aimed at a formidable target: public school segregation in America. Marshall argued that segregation was inherently unequal because it implied that government believed "Negroes [to be] inferior to all other human beings," and that it had a permanent, devastating effect on black children. In May 1954, a year and a half after he began his battle for Brown, Marshall had the joy of hearing Chief Justice Earl Warren read the Supreme Court's unanimous verdict: "In the field of public education the doctrine of 'separate but equal' has no place." School segregation had been declared unconstitutional.

Marshall's victory was marred by the news that his wife was fatally ill with cancer. Following her death in 1955, Marshall married a Hawaiian, Cecelia Suyat, with whom he eventually had two sons. During the seven years that followed his marriage, he waged to escape school desegregation, opposing southern attempts to ban the NAACP, lining up his forces to back the Reverend Martin Luther King, Jr., and vigorously defending civil rights demonstrators.

In September 1962, President John F. Kennedy appointed Marshall to the Second Circuit Court of Appeals. During his four years as a judge, Marshall ruled on a variety of cases, including the use of illegally obtained evidence in criminal trials, the deportation of aliens, and the First Amendment right to free expression. Not one of his 98 majority opinions was overturned by the Supreme Court. This remarkable record was in large part responsible for Marshall's 1965 appointment as U.S. solicitor general, a post never before held by a black citizen. During his two years as the nation's top-ranking courtroom advocate, Marshall won 14 of his 19 cases, most of them dealing with civil rights and privacy issues.

In 1967, Thurgood Marshall again made history when President Lyndon B. Johnson named him America's first black Supreme Court justice. In case after case, he defended individual rights and educational and legal equality for all races. After more than two decades of distinguished service as an Associate Justice, Marshall retired from the court in 1991.

Two years later, on January 24, 1993, Marshall died of heart failure at Bethdesda Naval Medical Center in Maryland. He was 84 years old.

At Marshall's funeral service, Chief Justice William H. Rehnquist said in his eulogy: "As a result of his career as a lawyer and as a judge, Thurgood Marshall left an indelible mark not just upon the law but upon his country. Inscribed above the front entrance to the Supreme Court building are the words 'Equal justice under law.' Surely no one individual did more to make these words a reality than Thurgood Marshall."

COLIN POWELL

Military leader Colin Powell was born in New York City on April 5, 1937. His father was a shipping clerk and his mother worked as a seamstress. Both parents, who had emigrated many years earlier from Jamaica, stressed the importance of education to Colin and his older sister, Marilyn.

Powell grew up in the Hunts Point section of the South Bronx and graduated from public high school there in 1954. He then enrolled at the City College of New York, where he majored in geology. The ambitious and energetic Powell also joined the Reserve Officers' Training Corps (ROTC), where he found that he thrived under military discipline. He became commander of the Pershing Rifles, the ROTC precision drill team, and graduated at the top of the college's ROTC class of 1958 with the rank of cadet colonel, the highest rank in the corps.

Upon graduation, Powell was commissioned a second lieutenant in the U.S. Army and went to West Germany after completing the necessary military training. There he helped to maintain a watch on the troops of the Warsaw Pact nations. He rose from platoon leader to commander of a rifle company. By 1960, when he returned to the United States, Powell was a first lieutenant—he had begun to climb the military ranks.

After several years of service, Powell was sent to South Vietnam as a military adviser to an infantry battalion in the early 1960s. Powell returned to South Vietnam for a second tour of duty in the late 1960s as a division operations officer. Wounded twice during his years in Vietnam, he was cited for bravery and received eleven medals for his service, including the Legion of Merit.

After returning to the United States, Powell enrolled in the graduate school of George Washington University in Washington, D.C., where he earned a master's degree in business administration in 1971. The following year Powell, who then held the rank of major, was appointed a White House Fellow. The fellowship sponsored promising military officers the opportunity to serve for a year in a department of the executive branch. This program was important to Powell because it helped officers who desired a career in policy-making. He was assigned to the staff of Frank C. Carlucci, then deputy director of the Office of Management and Budget (OMB). Both Carlucci and OMB director Caspar W. Weinberger were impressed with Powell and years later would hire him as their deputy.

During 1973 Powell served as a battalion commander in Korea. The following year he was appointed to a staff job at the Pentagon. In 1975 Powell, now a colonel, enrolled at the National War College. Before completing the course of study, he was assigned as the commander of the Second Brigade of the 101st Airborne Division at Fort Campbell, Kentucky. He returned to the War College in 1976 to graduate with distinction.

During the late 1970s Powell served as a military aide in the Department of Defense and as an assistant to the Secretary of Energy. After the election of President Ronald Reagan in 1980, Powell, now a major general, worked briefly as an aide to the new deputy secretary of defense, Frank Carlucci. Carlucci described Powell as "extraordinarily bright, articulate, and with excellent judgement." He said, "Nobody could provide you with better guidance . . . in the United States government." In 1981 Powell began two years of service as assistant commander of the Fourth Infantry Division at Fort Carson, Colorado. In the spring of 1983 Powell became deputy commander at Fort Leavenworth, Kansas, but he left this position in July to become senior military assistant to the secretary of defense, Caspar Weinberger.

Powell worked for Weinberger for three years, during which time he acquired a reputation as a skilled assistant who could expedite the flow of information and get along with different groups of people. He played an important role in several major military operations, including the U.S. invasion of Grenada in October 1983 and the 1986 raid on Libya.

In June 1986 Powell left the Department of Defense to assume another infantry command, this time as commanding general of the Fifth Corps, stationed in Frankfurt, Germany. However, six months later Powell was asked by Frank Carlucci, President Reagan's new national security adviser, to be Carlucci's deputy. Powell was reluctant to leave his military post for another civilian job, but President Reagan himself intervened and persuaded Powell to accept the offer.

Carlucci had succeeded Rear Admiral John Poindexter as national security adviser. Poindexter had been forced to resign after public disclosure of a secret arms deal with Iran, later known as the Iran-Contra scandal. General Powell was given the job of reorganizing the operations of the national security staff in line with the recommendations of the Tower Commission, which had been created by the president to investigate the scandal.

Powell proved once again that he was an efficient organizer who could work well with other people. Since he and Carlucci were alike in their approach to security policy, Carlucci often sent Powell to the White House to brief President Reagan. The personal relationship between Powell and Reagan grew, and in November 1987, when Carlucci succeeded Weinberger as secretary of defense, Reagan promoted Powell to national security adviser. Powell thus became the first African American to head the National Security Council.

In his new post Powell successfully coordinated the efforts of various technical advisers during the summit meeting in December 1987 between President Reagan and Russian leader Mikhail Gorbachev that led to the signing of the intermediate-range nuclear forces (INF) treaty. In the following months Powell had the responsibility of setting up an inspection program to make sure that the terms of the treaty were carried out. Despite existing rivalry among the involved government agencies, Powell worked out a cooperative effort with the Pentagon, the State Department, and the Arms Control and Disarmament Agency.

In August 1989 President George Bush nominated Powell to become chairman of the Joint Chiefs of Staff, the highest position of leadership in the nation's armed forces next to the president himself. In October, following his confirmation by the Senate, Powell became both the first African American and the youngest man to hold this important post.

Powell's skills as a military commander were soon needed. President George Bush and other government officials were angered by the international drug smuggling activities of General Manuel Noriega, the dictator of Panama. When Noriega's soldiers killed a U.S. marine in Panama, President Bush consulted with Powell, and both decided that the time had come to remove Noriega from power. As chairman of the Joint Chiefs, Powell had to see that the job was done.

In December 1989 Powell launched Operation Just Cause, an invasion of Panama by 26,000 U.S. troops. The operation was an enormous success: Noriega was quickly captured and brought to Florida for trial. He was later convicted on drug-trafficking charges and given a prison sentence.

In August 1990, when troops from Iraq invaded the neighboring country of Kuwait, Powell was again called upon by President Bush. Powell organized Operation Desert Shield, a deployment of 180,000 U.S. soldiers in Saudi Arabia, near the border that it shares with both Kuwait and Iraq. As both the United States and the United Nations demanded Iraq's withdrawal from Kuwait, Powell quietly made plans for an attack on Iraq, in cooperation with General H. Norman Schwarzkopf, head of U.S. forces in Saudi Arabia. Powell's major task was to coordinate the combined efforts of the United States and 17 other nations who had committed troops to the operation.

The U.N. Security Council ordered Iraqi leader Saddam Hussein to withdraw from Kuwait by January 15, 1991, or face military action. When Hussein ignored the deadline, Operation Desert Shield became Operation Desert Storm as multinational forces launched a massive air assault on Iraq. Following weeks of heavy bombing, a ground offensive began on February 24. Four days later Saddam Hussein, his army in shambles, agreed to withdraw from Kuwait.

Both Powell and Schwarzkopf were hailed as national heroes for leading the allied forces to victory in the Persian Gulf war. Powell was even considered as a likely candidate for vice-president in the 1992 election, but he told President Bush that he was not interested in becoming his running mate, choosing instead to remain as chairman of the Joint Chiefs of Staff, in which capacity he began to serve a new commander-in-chief, President Bill Clinton, in January 1993.

Powell's term as chairman of the Joint Chiefs of Staff ended eight months later, and so did his life in the military. Retiring from the U.S. Army made for a bittersweet time for him. Characteristically, he was looking forward to taking on new challenges. Yet he could not forget that he had been a soldier for more than 30 years and had enjoyed an honor-studded career that had carried him from the streets of the Bronx to the corridors of power in the nation's capital.

L. DOUGLAS WILDER

Politician Lawrence Douglas Wilder was born on January 17, 1931, in Richmond, Virginia, the seventh of eight children. His father was an insurance salesman and his mother worked as a maid. Wilder's grandparents on his father's side had married as slaves and then been separated; they were reunited after the Emancipation Proclamation of 1863.

Both of Wilder's parents paid close attention to his upbringing. His father was a strict disciplinarian, while his mother emphasized the importance of education and made him learn a new word every day. The family was poor but never went without food because they were able to grow and raise it themselves, despite the fact that they lived in the city.

Wilder attended segregated public schools in Richmond and earned spending money by doing various odd jobs, including shining shoes, washing windows, and operating an elevator. As a teenager he worked as a waiter in all-white Richmond hotels and clubs, where he was constantly exposed to racism. Years later he remembered racial jokes being told in his presence by diners, who treated him and other black personnel "like invisible men."

After graduating from high school in 1947, Wilder tried to enlist in the navy. However, he was only 16, and his mother refused to give the necessary permission. Instead he enrolled at Virginia Union College, an all-black institution in Richmond, and majored in chemistry. However, by the time he graduated in 1951 he had decided to become a lawyer.

Wilder's plans to enroll in law school were interrupted when he was drafted into the army to fight in the Korean War. He received the Bronze Star for valor—he braved enemy fire to rescue wounded troops—and later distinguished himself by forcing the surrender of a squad of enemy soldiers. When he and other black servicemen did not receive promotions for their efforts, Wilder filed a formal complaint with the government that led to more rapid recognition of African Americans in the armed services. Wilder ended his army service in 1953 with the rank of sergeant first class.

Wilder then returned to Richmond and was hired as a chemist by the state medical examiner's office. He spent most of his time running tests for alcohol levels in the blood. Wilder was impatient to begin the study of law, which the G.I. Bill would pay for, but he could not continue his studies in Virginia: at that time, blacks were banned from the state's law schools. In 1956 Wilder moved to Washington, D.C., and enrolled at the law school of Howard University, an all-black institution.

After graduating from Howard in 1959, Wilder returned to his old neighborhood in Richmond and set up a law practice. He specialized in criminal law and personal-injury cases, but because his clients were poor he found it difficult to earn a living. Wilder had to work hard to support himself and often took on too many clients. One of them sued Wilder for malpractice, claiming that the attorney had not given him adequate representation. As a consequence, Wilder was reprimanded by the Virginia Supreme Court for unprofessional conduct.

During the 1960s Wilder became involved in state politics as a spokesman for black causes, although he deliberately distanced himself from the national civil rights movement led by Martin Luther King, Jr. Although Wilder did not openly oppose King, privately he made it clear that he did not agree with

King's policy of nonviolence in working to end segregation.

Many blacks were upset by the remarks that Wilder made concerning racial issues. He said that blacks should stop making excuses and control their own destiny. Wilder told young people not to shun menial jobs, because any job is better than none. He said that blacks should accept some of the blame for the plight of their race.

In 1969 Wilder entered the race for a seat from Richmond in the state senate. The white vote was split among several white candidates, and Wilder was declared the winner. He became the first black elected to the Virginia legislature since the days of Reconstruction in the 19th century.

The Reverend Jesse Jackson, who knew Wilder in college, said: "The first time I met Doug, it was quickly apparent to me that he had his sights set on a goal higher than average. . . . We were just in fraternity politics then, but you could determine leadership traits and qualities."

As a state senator, Wilder cultivated a reputation as a confrontational, angry young black and often denounced racism from the senate floor. He became chairman of the important Privileges and Elections Committee and worked for legislation that would guarantee fair housing, labor union rights for public employees, and an increase in minority hiring by private businesses. Wilder also became known as an outspoken opponent of the death penalty, claiming that it was given far more often to blacks than to whites. Later he switched his position and became an advocate of the death penalty because he believed that blacks were being treated more fairly in the courts.

In July 1984 Wilder announced his candidacy for lieutenant governor of Virginia. By this time he had moderated his stand on other issues besides the death penalty and was no longer considered an outspoken liberal. Wilder campaigned throughout the state for the post for more than a year. He won the election in November 1985 with 51 percent of the vote, becoming the first African American to be elected to statewide office in Virginia.

Although the lieutenant governor's office is largely a ceremonial position, Wilder was sometimes called upon to make important decisions. In his official role of presiding over the state senate, he cast the tie-breaking vote that led to the establishment of a sex-education program in the state's schools. Wilder also served as chairman of the Drug Interdiction Task Force and chaired the National Democratic Lieutenant Governors Association.

For some time Wilder had been feuding privately with Charles Robb, the state Democratic leader who had been governor in the early 1980s. By 1986 their disagreements had become publicly known when some of Wilder's supporters accused Robb of secretly opposing the nomination of Wilder as lieutenant governor and offering only lukewarm support to his election campaign. Wilder himself began publicly criticizing the tax policies of the current governor, fellow Democrat Gerald Baliles.

Despite these intraparty wranglings, Baliles, Robb—now a U.S. senator—and Wilder had resolved their differences by the summer of 1989, and Wilder received the Democratic nomination for governor without opposition. His Republican opponent in the November election was J. Marshall Coleman, former state attorney general. Although Coleman was white, race was not discussed openly in the campaign. However, as the November election drew closer, Wilder occasionally drew attention in political speeches to his unique position as the first black candidate for governor of any state since Reconstruction.

The two major issues in the campaign were abortion rights and crime, especially drug-related offenses. Coleman supported a state constitutional amendment banning virtually all abortions, while Wilder was a strong defender of abortion rights. When Coleman accused Wilder of being "soft" on crime, Wilder proposed a tough antidrug program that he claimed he would personally supervise if elected.

On the eve of the election, Wilder appeared to have a comfortable lead. However, when returns were in, they showed Coleman losing by such a thin margin that a recount was ordered—the first statewide recount in Virginia history. The final tally declared Wilder the winner by less than 7,000 votes—one-third of one percent of the total cast.

Wilder immediately became a national political figure. He began making major speeches in other states, including New York, California, and Illinois—states with large numbers of electoral votes. Speculation immediately arose that Wilder was considering running for the U.S. presidency in 1992. In his speeches Wilder urged Democrats to move to the right politically, saying that they would recapture the White House only if they adopted a policy of "fiscal responsibility," stopped calling for tax increases, and reduced federal spending.

Speculation became reality in September 1991, when Wilder announced his candidacy for the Democratic presidential nomination. Meanwhile, he was having difficulty resolving financial problems in his own state. The Virginia economy was in decline, and the state government was faced with a severe loss of revenue that it needed for state services. Critics began referring to Wilder as an "absentee governor." In January 1992, four months after entering the presidential race, Wilder withdrew, saying that he needed to devote his full attention to governing the state of Virginia.

Douglas Wilder has made accomplishments that no other black man has. Speaking of the governor, Jesse Jackson said, "The people who are the first always have got to be overqualified, to be able to survive the double and triple standards, and obviously Doug was prepared to match those standards, to make a breakthrough." In 1993, Wilder announced his intention to pursue another first—becoming the first black man to be elected to the U.S. Senate from Virginia.

Blanche K. Bruce

Christopher, Maurine. *America's Black Congressmen*. New York: Thomas Y. Crowell, 1971.

St. Clair, Sadie Daniel. *The National Career of Blanche Kelso Bruce*. New York: New York University Press, 1947.

Ralph Bunche

Haskins, James. *Ralph Bunche: A Most Reluctant Hero*. New York: Hawthorn Books, 1974.

Mann, Peggy. *Ralph Bunche: U.N. Peacemaker*. New York: Coward, McCann & Geoghegan, 1975.

Rivlin, Benjamin, ed. *Ralph Bunche: The Man and His Times*. New York: Holmes & Meir, 1990.

Shirley Chisholm

Chisholm, Shirley. *The Good Fight*. New York: Harper & Row, 1973.

———. *Unbought and Unbossed*. New York: Houghton Mifflin, 1970.

Sceader, Catherine. *Shirley Chisholm: Teacher and Congresswoman*. Hillside, NJ: Enslow, 1990.

Benjamin O. Davis, Sr., and Benjamin O. Davis, Jr.

Davis, Benjamin O., Jr. *Benjamin O. Davis, Jr., American: An Autobiography*. Washington, D.C.: Smithsonian Institution, 1991.

Fletcher, Marvin. *America's First Black General: Benjamin O. Davis, Sr., 1880–1970*. Kansas: University Press of Kansas, 1989.

William H. Hastie

Ware, Gilbert. *William Hastie: Grace Under Pressure*. New York: Oxford University Press, 1984.

Thurgood Marshall

Aldred, Lisa. *Thurgood Marshall*. New York: Chelsea House, 1990.

Haskins, James. *Thurgood Marshall: A Life for Justice*. New York: H. H. Holt, 1992.

Hess, Debra. *Thurgood Marshall: The Fight for Equal Justice*. Englewood Cliffs, NJ: Silver Burdett Press, 1992.

Colin Powell

Adler, Bill. *The Generals: The New American Heroes*. New York: Avon Books, 1991.

Binkin, Martin, and Mark J. Eitelberg. *Blacks in the Military*. Washington, D.C.: Brookins Institution, 1982.

Brown, Warren. *Colin Powell*. New York: Chelsea House, 1992.

L. Douglas Wilder

Baker, Donald P. *Wilder: Hold Fast to Dreams*. Cabin John, MD: Seven Locks Press, 1989.

Edds, Margaret. *Claiming the Dream: the Victorious Campaign of Douglas Wilder of Virginia*. Chapel Hill, NC: Algonquin Books of Chapel Hill, 1990.

Yancey, Dwayne. *When Hell Froze Over: The Untold Story of Doug Wilder, a Black Politician's Rise to Power in the South*. Dallas: Taylor Publishing, 1990.

PICTURE CREDITS

RICHARD RENNERT has edited the nearly 100 volumes in Chelsea House's award-winning BLACK AMERICANS OF ACHIEVEMENT series, which tells the stories of black men and women who have helped shape the course of modern history. He is also the author of several sports biographies, including *Henry Aaron*, *Jesse Owens*, and *Jackie Robinson*. He is a graduate of Haverford College in Haverford, Pennsylvania.